THE GIFT OF

GRIT

Unleash the Power of Passion & Perseverance, Rewire Your Beliefs, Build Resilience, and Achieve Your Long-term Goals

SOM BATHLA
www.sombathla.com/amazon

Your Free Gift

As a token of my thanks for taking out time to read my book, I would like to offer you a free gift:

Click Below and Download your **Free Report**

Learn 5 Mental Shifts To Turbo-Charge Your Performance In Every Area Of Your Life - in Next 30 Days!

You can also grab your FREE GIFT Report through this below URL:

http://sombathla.com/mentalshifts

Table of Contents

More Books by Som Bathla

The Magic Of Accelerated Learning

The Power of Self Discipline

The Science of High Performance

The Way To Lasting Success

The Mindful Mind

Conquer Your Fear Of Failure

The Mindset Makeover

Living Beyond Self Doubt

Focus Mastery

Just Get It Done

You may also visit my all books together at http://sombathla.com/amazon

Introduction

"Grit is passion and perseverance for very long-term goals. Grit is having stamina. Grit is sticking with your future, day-in, day-out. Not just for the week, not just for the month, but for years. And working really hard to make that future a reality. Grit is living life like it's a marathon, not a sprint."

~ Angela Duckworth

My friend, Geni, embodies the essence of grit.

She is the eldest of 5 children and grew up in a poor developing country. The year Geni turned 18, her mother died while giving birth to her brother. Since her father was only employed part-time, Geni had to step up and provide for her family.

Despite having two full-time jobs at a factory and at a doctor's clinic, she finished college on a full scholarship. Oftentimes, she had to skip meals so she could have enough cash to buy rice for her younger brothers and sisters. Her whole family lived in the basement of a shack in the slum part of town. The basement often flooded during the rainy season. All sorts of garbage, excrement, and debris would make it onto her family's living room.

Throughout her life, she was dismissed or laughed at by her neighbors and even relatives for "wasting her time" getting a college education. They told her she should just get married and let her "no good" siblings fend for themselves.

But she didn't pay any attention to what people said about her. She kept her family together and provided for them by putting off getting married until she was well into her thirties. Today, Geni lives in a big metropolitan city, the proud mother of an engineer son and an attorney daughter. She owns two homes and has retired comfortably.

At any point, Geni could have easily quit. After all, she had more than enough excuses to quit. She could have easily justified giving up and taking the easy way out by getting married as a teenager. Her family was broke. Her parents and grandparents had never seen the inside of a college. Her mother died early. Her father was almost always never around. One of her siblings was constantly in and out of jail. She lived in a community where pursuing a college education or even speaking English was viewed as being "uppity" and "pretentious".

Despite the total lack of support, her depressing environment, and gnawing insecurities, she stayed focused on her dream of getting a college degree. After long years of college— which were often interrupted by very demanding work schedules and frequent family emergencies—she earned that college education she has had her eye on since she was a little girl.

Why did Geni succeed when there are countless other "Genis" out there who quit on their dreams and quietly faded into a background of poverty, misery, and anonymity?

What did Geni have that other people in her situation didn't?

Well, it wasn't her IQ. She had a fairly average IQ. It wasn't her ability. It wasn't her EQ either. EQ, of course, involves the ability to emotionally read other people and get along smoothly at all times. In fact, she is quite a bit of a wallflower – a true introvert. Although not exactly a dull student, Geni was not the sharpest tool in the shed. Painfully shy, she wasn't exactly the life of the party. Regardless, she was able to become successful enough to move all her family members to a metropolitan city to enjoy comfortable middle-class lives.

What is her secret?

It was GRIT. She simply hung on despite how hard things got. She remained motivated regardless of how many people told her she would fail or wouldn't amount to much. Regardless of whatever negativity people had for her, her family, her neighborhood, she kept keeping on. She stayed focused on her ultimate goals even when she felt she was running on empty.

What is Grit?

Grit, it turns out, is the secret ingredient to success. No matter how smart you are, no matter how many advantages you were born with, and no matter how great you are with people, chances are, if you don't have grit, you're going to have a tough time on the road to success.

Grit is defined as having perseverance despite challenging environments, negative feedback, as well as setbacks and failures on the road to your goals. People with grit are able to succeed despite the fact that they often suffer from internal roadblocks like low self-confidence and low self-esteem.

According to research by psychologist Angela Duckworth, grit is the **ability to stay passionate enough to persevere while chasing after long-term goals**. This perseverance of effort promotes the overcoming of obstacles that lie on the road to accomplishment and acts as a catalyst to achieving of long-term goals.

Think of grit as your ability to stay pumped up as you run a marathon. It's easy to think that you're going to finish the race in the first thirteen miles of a marathon, but as the race drags on, doubts start to creep in. Your muscles start to get tired. You become really sweaty. It gets really hot, and your mind is flooded with so many thoughts telling you to quit. But if you have grit, you remain as passionate on Mile 26 as you were on Mile 1. You stay pumped up all the way to the finish line.

Grit is living life like it's a marathon, not a sprint.

The Essence of Grit

Grit involves having long-term stamina. That's really what it boils down to because you have to have emotional and mental stamina to keep on trying even when the rewards you anticipated aren't coming soon enough.

In certain stages of your path to success, the rewards you expected are nowhere to be seen. It would be great if you could see the outlines on the horizon, but they're completely absent from the landscape. Your ability to put one foot in front of the other, so to speak, as you move to that horizon requires grit. In other words, you have the ability to keep your eyes on the prize day after day and for years to come.

Grit means focusing on the long-term goal and seeing the big picture. You see everything in context. The step you're taking today toward that horizon that doesn't immediately show your ultimate objective is understood as part of the process.

You automatically assume that even if you can't see the ultimate goal from where you stand now, this all has a purpose. In the back of your mind, you know this will lead to your hopes and dreams. You are able to make that connection despite the huge amount of time that needs to pass before you achieve your goal.

Grit Doesn't Just Involve Patience

By this point, you might be thinking that grit sounds similar to patience. After all, patience simply means hanging on to a process and doing what you need to do until enough time has passed and your reward materializes.

It's actually more than that. Grit doesn't just involve the ability to keep pushing forward as you wait for the ultimate reward. It doesn't just involve keeping your eyes trained on a long-term vision. It **also includes the ability, willingness, and commitment to work hard to make that very long-term future a reality**. Anybody can be patient. They can basically just sit back and wait for time to pass.

Grit involves patience, but you're taking massive actions while you are waiting. You're putting in the work. You're taking chances and exploring opportunities. You are learning what you need to learn so when the opportunity presents itself, you get closer and closer to your long-term goal.

The Sad Reality

Unfortunately, the current educational system in most countries is not geared toward building grit. In fact, the majority of the population is completely clueless regarding this success factor. While most elementary schools in the United States are equipped to measure IQ, they are unprepared to determine, much less encourage, the formation of grit.

With this as a background, it doesn't help that the modern society and culture increasingly views success as a sprint, not a marathon. In other words, we run the very real risk of setting kids up for failure, because we do not adequately prepare them for the long, bruising journey ahead to ultimate success.

It doesn't matter how you define success. Maybe you're thinking of becoming an attorney, a physician, founding a successful internet startup, or maybe you have your eyes on an academic career. Whatever the case may be, big dreams often require long time horizons and a steady investment of effort and analysis.

In other words, success is a persistent, long journey just like a marathon. You have to keep moving toward your goal regardless of what you feel like. Maybe you're feeling crabby, maybe you're feeling discouraged because somebody said something bad to you. But you still have to put one foot in front of the other to eventually reach where you want to go. That's what grit is all about.

But unfortunately, most educational systems don't teach students how to build grit. This book is written with an objective to list out the necessary elements and steps needed to build grit, so you can harness the power of passion and perseverance to reach your long- term goals.

How Do We Build Grit?

Do you want the real answer? Well, honestly, there is no direct answer to it. That's the state of the science.

However, there are circumstantial approaches to building grit, and I will guide you through these later in this book. If you are looking for a direct, pure answer as to a laser-focused, clinical approach to developing grit, the state of psychological studies across the world is all over the place. It's a confusing mess, so there is really no direct answer.

Instead, we approximate the answer circumstantially. First, we'll discuss and focus on the things that don't build grit. Grit has little to do with your talent, your starting potential, your IQ, or your background. In fact, people with no talent, absolutely no starting potential, low or mediocre IQ, impoverished backgrounds and a family history of physical, sexual and mental abuse have succeeded immensely, thanks to grit.

The key takeaway here is that the common initial indicators of success simply do not apply.

Frustrated yet? Well, here's the thing. As exasperating as all this may seem, this is actually good news. Why? Grit is a choice. Seriously. It is not imposed on us by circumstances we can't control.

I don't know about you, but certain things will always apply universally to everyone, irrespective of who you are. For instance, you can't choose your parents. You can't choose your upbringing, you can't choose the neighborhood you were born into, and you definitely can't choose your IQ.

Therefore, grit is really good news because it involves a choice. Regardless of where we come from, what we look like, regardless of our gender, we can choose to develop grit.

It is not a product of the accident or birth, nor is it imposed from the outside on us by forces beyond our control. It's not like somebody can point a gun at your head and force you to be successful. It's a choice. It's a mindset that we actively pick to cultivate.

This book teaches you how to cultivate grit, so you can find the sustained focus and the willpower you need to achieve victory for the long-term. Grit is the ultimate tool for delayed gratification, which, as you should already know, leads to greater rewards in life.

With that, let's start now and move to Chapter 1.

Chapter 1: GRIT: The Strongest Predictor of Success

****

"Nothing in this world can take the place of persistence. Talent will not: nothing is more common than unsuccessful men with talent. Genius will not; unrewarded genius is almost a proverb. Education will not: the world is full of educated derelicts. Persistence and determination alone are omnipotent."

~ Calvin Coolidge

You're probably wondering by now, what is it about grit that separates it from other traditional indicators of success? You might be thinking what about all the other factors you've been hearing, claiming that they lead to your success.

It's easy to see how IQ can lead to greater achievement. After all, the ability to comprehend new information quickly and tie it into your existing knowledge base can give you a tremendous competitive advantage. Similarly, being able to deal smartly with people can enable you to accomplish a high degree of organic leadership that can open up many opportunities for you. But by now you'd have understood already that grit doesn't involve any of these.

Then what makes it so special? What accounts for its potency? Is it some recent breakthrough invention that has some magical impact on your success?

For that let's try to go deeper and understand the genesis of this. The term grit was popularized by researcher Angela Duckworth through her research on the subject followed by her great book named *Grit: The Power of Passion and Perseverance*, but history[1] shows that the ideals of **persistence** and **tenacity** have existed as virtues since Aristotle. In modern times, the concept of grit can be tracked

---

1

https://esource.dbs.ie/bitstream/handle/10788/3338/hdip_brown_y_2017.pdf?sequence=1&isAllowed=y

back to Galton who in 1889 wrote that the most eminent individuals in society are typically blessed with **talent, zeal** and a **capacity for hard labor**. Cox (1926) later identified common traits of 300 geniuses highlighting their **perseverance, tenacity,** and **doggedness**. The 1985 study 'Success in College' continued this vein of thought demonstrating evidence that **purposeful, continuous commitment** to certain activities was the best predictor of success in college (Willingham, 1985).

Therefore, grit – perseverance with passion to stick to long-term goals, isn't entirely a new concept, persistence and tenacity have already been identified as the key tenets for achievement.

What Duckworth has contributed to the modern world is the depth of research evidencing how grit trumps all other factors, when it comes to long-term adherence to your goals.

In one of her studies at United States Military Academy, a four-year training academy famously known as West Point

Military, she studied 1,200 new cadets to assess the factors which predict who stayed in military training and which ones dropped out. The new cadets training for the first-years is known as "Beast Barracks", which is a seven-week infamous training in which they'd toil in the classroom and on the field for 17 hours every day without a break. Many would drop out. Duckworth wanted to find out why some cadets managed to endure this challenge, while others just gave up.

In her book, she writes that researchers had been trying to solve this puzzle for more than fifty years. But even the school's best means of screening its applicants— known as Whole Candidate Score, a weighted mixture of a student's scholastic assessment test (SATs, high school ranking, leadership ability, and physical fitness— does not anticipate who will succeed and who will fail at training. Even with such a rigorous admissions process, about 1 in 20 cadets drop out during the summer of training before their first academic year.

So Duckworth designed her own way of scoring candidates, giving each a questionnaire that tested their willingness to persevere in pursuit of long-term goals. The questionnaire was to test the level of grit of the cadets. The cadets' survey answers helped predict whether they would make it through the grueling program or quit sooner. In fact, it was a much better predictor than the Whole Candidate Score. While on the other hand the Whole Candidate Score actually had no predictive relationship with whether you would drop out that summer (although it was the best predictor of later grades, military performance, and physical performance),

She also analyzed results from the National Spelling Bee contest (an annual spelling bee event in the US, in which contestants are asked to spell a broad selection of words, usually with a varying degree of difficulty) to determine which children were more likely to advance and which were not. In another study, Duckworth partnered with a private corporation and surveyed managers to determine which sales representatives would be more likely to leave the company and which ones would be successful.

Duckworth analyzed data from first-year inner-city elementary school teachers to measure those who wouldn't return after that first year and, of those who would, which ones would be most effective at making sure students met their outcomes.

In Duckworth's various cross-sectional studies on long-term success, she found out that grit, when factoring for every other element, outweighed other traditional success factors like social intelligence, looks, IQ, and physical health. Indeed, grit even helps people overcome background factors like family income, family educational attainment, scores on standardized tests, as well as physical safety at school.

Therefore, according to Duckworth, grit is a better indicator of long-term success than all other factors. Despite the seeming differences of these subject groups in different studies, she found out that grit was the primary indicator of whether a person will make it all the way through a process. Gritty people put consistent efforts and do it with perseverance. Another study on expert performers in diverse domains found that thousands of hours of extremely effortful deliberate practice is prerequisite for achieving world-class levels of skill.

There was a famous quote by Woody Allen saying: *"80 percent of success is just showing up"*.

If we combine the showing up argument with skill development through highly effortful deliberate focused practice, then it can be argued that grit predicts high achievement by inclining individuals to both show up and work very hard, continuously, toward a highly valued goal for years and even decades.

How Grit Overpowers Your IQ, EQ and other Factors?

Now let's talk more specifically about IQ and EQ. I'd hate to report this, but IQ is hardwired and strongly influenced primarily by your genetics and environment. If you come from parents who have high IQ scores, chances are, you would have a high IQ score as well. Unfortunately, if your parents are fairly low on the IQ charts, you may have a slightly higher IQ than them, but your IQ improvement is pretty much determined by the starting IQ base of your parents.

Based on wide-ranging and long-term studies[2], scientists conclude that somewhere around 50% of the natural variation in IQ can be attributed to genetics, the rest is due to other factors, primarily environmental. Another study[3] conducted on 164 eight-grader students revealed that self-discipline outdoes IQ in predicting academic performance of adolescents. Similarly, another important factor namely emotional quotient or EQ is also picked up from your background, life experiences as well as from genetics.

Fortunately, you don't have any of these problems with grit. IQ, EQ and other factors are not entirely under your control and somewhat hardwired. Either you're born with money or you're not. Either you're born in a great neighborhood or you're not. Grit sidesteps all of that because it's a choice.

[2] https://ghr.nlm.nih.gov/primer/traits/intelligence
[3] http://journals.sagepub.com/doi/abs/10.1111/j.1467-9280.2005.01641.x

You can choose to be gritty even if you live in a slum. You can choose to be gritty when you are surrounded by people who have low IQs. You can choose to be gritty even when so many people are telling you to give up or are telling you that you do not have what it takes.

Whatever hopes and dreams you may have, they can come to a quick and early death, largely because of the environment they're in. It takes an iron will. In other words, it takes a tremendous amount of grit to overcome the daily programming of negativity surrounding you. For example, if you have a dream of making millions of dollars every year, it's very easy to succumb to the negativity of broke people around you. It's hard to soar like an eagle when you are surrounded by turkeys. And unfortunately, if you do not have grit, it's very easy to be dragged down and held back by your environment. This is why grit blows away other common explanations for success.

Therefore, it's worth emphasizing here that things like IQ, talent, a nurturing background, a social background, social indicators, the ready availability of opportunities, and even self-discipline (explained with research later) do not come close to predicting long-term success as grit.

Grit is Purely a Personal Choice

Grit really boils down to choosing to hang on to your dreams. It really boils down to a conscious daily decision to keep investing actions and choices to your ultimate goal. It is distinctly yours. Nobody can be gritty for you. It is something you choose every day. It is not determined by immutable factors.

Accordingly, grit is a reflection of who you are. It reflects what's important to you, it tells the world what you are willing to sacrifice for. It is distinctly your own. This is why it's potent. Because people can take away your possessions. Disasters can take away a lot of the things you hold dear. But until you give up on yourself, you can always choose to hang on to grit. You can always choose to refuse to let external factors deny you your hopes and dreams.

There are many stories of millionaires who—through one bad choice or another—became impoverished overnight. All their millions, or even billions, go up in smoke overnight. But guess what happens? Interestingly enough, a significant percentage of millionaires who declare bankruptcy become millionaires again.

What this highlights is that it's not really their millions in the bank that made them millionaires. It's not the advantages they have. Instead, it's something else. It is their internal focus, it is their internal decision-making process and, ultimately, it's their willingness to hang on to their vision of themselves. It's their grit—their perseverance and passion for their long-term goals—which kick them to bounce back. They obviously see themselves as being millionaires. And the fact that they may be broke or even in the hole doesn't take this inner vision away.

And what do you think happens to them every day? That's right, they feed that vision not just by hoping and wishing that somehow, some way, it comes to pass. Instead, they take directed actions that lead to that ultimate conclusion. It obviously isn't happening overnight, but they're investing their time, focus and decisions toward that goal. Not only are they emotionally and mentally engaged, but they are also taking directed physical actions that lead them closer and closer to that alternate reality.

Let's put it this way, they don't beat themselves up feeling sorry for themselves. They don't think of themselves as victims. They don't feel sorry for themselves. Instead, they are all too eager to get back up after they've gotten knocked down.

There are actually many millionaires who went through serial bankruptcies[4]. That's right. Somebody who made millions of dollars, went bankrupt and everything went back to zero, then they became a millionaire again. Mind blowing, right? Well, if that person did not have the right values and was not focused on the right goals, it only takes one massive hit for that person to just give up.

Just on a related note, it was quite intriguing to research that becoming a millionaire isn't that hard, at least that's what the available research number shows. According to recent figures by research firm SPECTREM[5], there are on record, as of 2018, nearly 10 million millionaires in the United States. That's a lot of people, considering the US has a population of roughly around 300 million. Roughly 1 in 30. That's not too shabby, right?

Once again, grit is a personal choice. That regardless of how bitter your experience was, and regardless of how big a fool you think you have become because of your bad choices, you choose to keep pursuing your dream. You never succumb to the idea that you're too old, you're too dumb, you just don't have what it takes or the world is just not going to give you the success that you deserve. You don't entertain any of that. You just keep seeing the vision.

---

[5] https://spectrem.com/Content/press-release-new-spectrem-group-market-insights-report-reveals-significant-growth-in-US-household-wealth-in-2017.aspx

Grit really boils down to your willingness to grab your personal reality and own your life. Because the moment you blame other people for whatever failures or frustrations you have, you're actually giving them your life. Think about that for a second.

Think about it, if you say that the reason why you're poor and miserable is because of what Joe Blow did to you, then it logically follows that, since Joe Blow caused the problem, he also has the solution. Now, when you hand the solution to somebody else that you cannot control, you have effectively given up on your life. I know that sounds extreme, but it's absolutely true.

If you look at the people around who are struggling in life, whether financially, socially or just are walking around with tremendous guilt and regret, what do they all have in common? They feel they are not in control of their lives. They feel there's some sort of past trauma or people who are to blame for why they are frustrated, why they are struggling, and why they cannot have the best things in life.

What they have actually done is they have given the ability to fix their problem to somebody else by blaming that person. Now, let me tell you, it's hard enough to try to change yourself, can you imagine trying to change somebody else? Sadly, that is the kind of impossible position you put yourself in when you choose to blame other people for what's wrong with your life. Thinking like a victim is a one-way ticket to a life not worth living. You have a choice right now to stop blaming and to start taking ownership of the big vision you have for yourself.

If you're not making the kind of money that you would like to make, you have a decision to make today. If you don't have the kind of marriage you would like, you have a decision to make today. If you are unhealthy or you feel that you're out of shape, you have a decision to make today. Nobody can make that decision for you.

And the secret to all of this is setting a goal and sticking to it. Despite the fact that you have a mediocre IQ, despite the fact that you don't have advantages, despite the fact that it seems like things just won't work out for you, regardless of that, you can choose to set your sights on that goal and do whatever is necessary, for however long it takes, until you get there.

Effort Counts Twice in Grit's Equation

When you exercise grit, you don't sit patiently and wait for circumstances to improve for taking action. Instead, you get out in the street and start putting all your efforts. The characteristics of gritty people vis-à-vis others is that not only they put in long hours, thanks to their passions and clarity of goals, but they put more qualitative efforts into what they do. If they realize that they lack some skill or knowledge to handle the work better, they strive hard to master that skill, so they execute better actions toward their goals.

They know the importance of putting in the efforts on a consistent basis. Researcher Duckworth has put it succinctly that effort counts twice and offers below equation to capture the essence of grit.

*Talent X **Effort** = Skill*

*Skill X **Effort** = Achievement.*

Of course, talent is important for achievement, but putting effort is twice as important. If you have talent, then investing efforts will ensure that you will quickly improve skill. But you don't stop there, you have to put in the effort again to generate a productive outcome through application of the skill.

Take the example of a super "talented" "genius" who puts in no effort. What do you get? Nothing, really—just a disappointed genius! Alternatively, you can have a modestly talented individual who hustles and keeps putting in efforts. You get it. This is the sure short recipe for extraordinary achievement.

Someone might argue that the equation of success can't be so straightforward. Yes, I agree, there are lot many factors that play a role. You may have different upbringing, a disadvantageous social support system, or simply not so encourage ecosystem. All these factors play a role, and success is not merely a game governed by your internal traits, you have to deal with outside realities as well to achieve something big in the material world.

But, what 'efforts counts twice' theory suggests is that when you consider individuals in identical circumstances, what each achieves depends on just two things, talent, and effort. Talent—how fast we can improve a skill—absolutely plays a vital role; it matters. But effort factors into the calculations twice, not once. Effort builds skill. At the very same time, effort makes skill productive.

Gritty people know this formula, and they keep putting efforts toward their goals.

How Gritty Are You?

You might be wondering, where you stand in terms of grittiness.

Where do you find yourself on grit level? Based on your life experiences and behavior, actions, or decisions, you've taken in your life, can you honestly tell if you had been gritty or not so? Are you interested to explore further?

Duckworth has formulated a grit questionnaire to help you assess your "Grit Score". It has 10 questions asking you about your thoughts, behaviors, and actions in different situations of life. Once you answer the questions, you will get your Grit Score. You can test your own level of grit by checking this Grit Scale[6]

Now let's move on to the next section of the book, where we understand the subtle differences grit has when compared to self-discipline and resilience. You will also learn how grit is even more important than these other non-cognitive traits.

[6] https://angeladuckworth.com/grit-scale/

Chapter 2: Grit Outperforms Self-Discipline & Resilience

****

"Grit is not just having resilience in the face of failure, but also having deep commitments that you remain loyal to over many years."

~ Angela Duckworth

Grit vs. Self-Discipline

You might be thinking that grit sounds suspiciously similar to the ability to control one's impulses i.e. self-discipline. As you've probably heard, if you want to be successful in any way, shape or form, you have to have the ability to control yourself. This means you're not going to let your emotions get the better of you when you're making a decision. This also means you're going to have a long-term view of a particular decision.

We are always given a choice between doing things that pay off immediately or belatedly. For example, laziness pays off instantly. Working hard, on the other hand, pays off in the end. You can choose to play video games or you can choose to study for law school admissions. You can choose to go drinking with your buddies or you can spend time preparing your medical school application. I hope you see the dichotomy here in regards to quick payoffs.

Delayed gratification is all about having a long enough view of the future so that you realize that by avoiding instant payoffs now and putting in the work, you stand to gain better rewards in the future. While you may not have a good time now because you're not going out drinking or doing drugs with your friends, it pays off tremendously once you finish your education for CPA or a law school and you're making $200,000 a year working for a big corporate house.

In other words, you have an idea of the massive difference between payoffs you can enjoy today and payoffs that scale exponentially over time when you choose to work on your future today. That's delayed gratification.

And this is where the confusion comes in because a lot of people are thinking that delayed gratification and the self-discipline that it requires is the same as grit. While it is true that self-discipline is crucial to delayed gratification and delayed gratification usually leads to success, this is not the same as grit. While you must regulate your focus, desires, and actions despite whatever temptations you face or the shortcuts that materialize, this is not grit.

Self-discipline is required on a day to day basis. It plays out on a micro level. Either you did something pleasurable, but leads to very shallow rewards, or you did something fairly uncomfortable or inconvenient, which leads to greater rewards that scale up over time. That's the kind of choice you make when you are exercising self-discipline in the context of delayed gratification. This happens day to day on an immediate level. Either you delay gratification today, or you don't. Each day you delay gratification, however, the success that you stand to collect in the future gets bigger and bigger.

The key difference between self-discipline and grit is that self-discipline involves *immediacy*. **Self-discipline is immediate**. It has to happen right now because you're either delaying your gratification right now or you're not. **Grit, on the other hand, is long-term and focuses on the big picture**. It is the ability to stick to your goals and commitment to action despite setbacks.

Self-control is required when there is a conflict between two possible action tendencies (i.e., impulses)—one corresponding to a momentarily alluring but unworthy goal and the other corresponding to a more valued goal whose benefits are deferred in time, in distant future.

If you notice it more closely, self-control and grit both involve safeguarding of valued goals in the face of adversity. Where they principally differ is in (A) the types of goals that are being defended, (B) the nature of the adversities; and (C) the timescale involved.

Self-control is required to adjudicate between lower-level goals entailing necessarily conflicting actions. One cannot eat one's cake and have it later, too. In contrast, grit entails staying loyal or committed to a highest-level goal over long stretches of time and in the face of disappointments and setbacks. It follows that self-control is more tightly coupled with everyday success, whereas grit is more tightly coupled with exceptional achievements that often take decades—or even an entire lifetime—to accomplish.

What follows therefore in gritty people is that even if you experience crushing disappointments today, you are able to get back up and try again. You get knocked back down, you try again. You keep repeating this over and over for however long it takes until you achieve your goal.

How are you able to do this? Well, it's because you always see the big picture. You see that your immediate failure does not define you. The more steps you take toward your goal, the smaller and smaller that setback becomes in the rearview mirror of your life. Grit is all about focusing on the big picture windshield in front of you. It is the ability to stick to that picture. You get thrown off, but grit brings your attention back to your goal's direction.

It's kind of like a **personal GPS system**. The last time you used a GPS, this probably happened to you. You were going to a spot on the map, but maybe you made a wrong turn, or you stopped by some grocery store. The moment you did that, the GPS system told you that it was recalculating, so it came up with another route. Grit is like your internal GPS. You may have made a wrong decision, which could have taken you further away from your goal. It may hurt, you may feel like a fool, but grit returns your focus to where you need to go. So, sooner or later, with enough action and more decisions on your part, you get closer and closer to your goal.

In the nutshell, grit enables you to always keep your ultimate success in mind. Grit involves simple focus. You know where you're oriented, so that even when disaster strikes, you still find your way toward your goal. And it has a large scale view. Grit always keeps your main focus in mind so that even if you get knocked down, you still find your way there.

You might not immediately move in that direction—maybe you lost a large amount of money, maybe you got divorced, maybe you got thrown in jail—those often take time to resolve. But grit still keeps your focus on the big picture. And sooner or later, you find yourself headed in that direction.

Ideally, you should have both self-discipline and grit for success, and that will create an amazing life worth quoting. But if I were forced to choose only one, I would choose grit. Because grit always reminds me that there is this big goal. And regardless of how I fail in the short-term, regardless of how badly I get tempted and distracted, I keep finding myself going back.

Grit is the key to ultimate success because you don't have to be a genius. You don't have to be a rocket scientist. You don't have to be born into money. You don't have to be surrounded by the very best in your field. **You just have to stick to the plan**.

Therefore, I choose grit over self-control, if someone asks me to choose one. But the ideal thing to do is to focus on developing both.

How is Grit different from Resilience?

Resilience involves the ability to get back up when you've been knocked down or to come back fighting stronger after a loss. And you'd say grit also means to keep pushing further after every failure. So what's the difference?

There is a subtle difference. While the end results for both resilience and grit are same, it means keep moving forward despite adversities and failures, the *minute difference lies in the driving force behind each*.

Resilience is the outlook of optimism to continue when you've experienced some failures and times are so tough that others see continuing as futile or impossible. Here the driving force is your outlook toward the life, you take things in a positive way, and therefore keep moving. On the other hand, grit attaches emotions with it—it is the motivational drive that keeps you on a difficult task over a sustained period of time. **Grit pulls you because you are passionate about things**. Grit doesn't simply means getting up after every fall, it has additional element of motivation attached to it.

In these two sections, you learned how grit is important for achieving long-term success, and why this overpowers other non-cognitive traits of humans. The objective was to give you enough convincing thoughts on the importance of grit, before we talk about how to develop grit.

Now let's move onto the next chapter to learn how to build grit.

Chapter 3: 6 Steps To Build Personal Grit

****

"Grit is that mix of passion, persistence, perseverance, and self-discipline that keeps us moving forward in spite of obstacles. It's not flashy, and that's precisely the point. In a world in which we're frequently distracted by sparkly displays of skill, grit makes the difference in the long run."

~Daniel Coyle

In this chapter, I'm going to give you an overview of how you can build grit. Again, to recap what we discussed earlier, there is no official, scientific, bulletproof way to build grit. And this should come as no surprise because grit ultimately is a choice and it's personal, as I've already emphasized enough at start of this book. That, in itself, should tell you that there is no one size fits all solution to building grit. There is no one path that would work for all people at all times, in all circumstances.

Instead, the framework that you're going to follow to build grit must take into account what's special or different with your life. In other words, you have to take full ownership of it. You have to customize it and mix and match it with whatever else is going on in your life as well as your past experiences. However, before you move ahead to list out the framework or steps to build grit, let's understand what is considered as must have to build grit.

Prerequisites for Building Grit:

The gritty people have four psychological assets necessary in common, as researcher Duckworth suggests. They strive to cultivate these four things namely interest, practice, purpose, and hope.

1. Interest: You need to be intrinsically drawn to something— that means that something should pull you toward it. It's because you're not going to put in the required, sustained effort if you're only and just interested in something or you're doing it merely because someone else wants you to do it. You need to have a passionate interest. There are two kinds of passions 'firework' passion and 'compass' passion. While the former passion is just sporadic, it comes and goes, on the other hand, the compass passion is something that guides you through life. You need to have compass passion toward what you want to achieve. The grittiest people have something they love to do.

2. Practice: Passion alone isn't enough. You can't passionately sit and just read more and more about what you are passionate about. You need to put the real work every day—that means Every. Single. Day. You need to design your life around your passion—that's what gritty people do. You must be ready to improve your skills, regardless of how well you currently perform. Gritty people know that to achieve their Big Hairy Audacious Goals (BHAGs), as Jim Collin states, they need to become expert and masters in whatever they do.

3. Purpose: Without purpose, one may not be able to carry on their interest for a long time. Gritty people have a purpose much bigger them themselves. If you want a mature passion and sustainable grit, your purpose needs to be bigger than yourself. You can't be motivated enough for life, if your purpose is just to show-off your six-pack abs or clicking selfies with your new big house or car. The purpose that is limited to only you is not the cup of tea for gritty people. Gritty people dare to dream about putting impacting society in some way . They think about changing the lives of people, finding the way to inspire millions to lead their life with joy. The bigger the purpose, the stronger the grit. It's essential to identify how their work is connected to their own wellbeing and the wellbeing of others.

4. Hope: On the path to becoming a gritty person, you will often bump your heads and fall down. Hope plays a significant role in the journey to becoming gritty. It's the rising-to-the-occasion type of perseverance in which we know we have the ability to achieve what we want. We need to have hope. We need to see the future can be better than our present, and we need to believe we have the power to make it so if we put in the required effort. People lose their grit when they are unable to get back up after a setback. But when we get back up, it prevails.

The combination of Interest + Practice + Purpose + Hope as ingredients is the solid recipe to prepare a solid gritty dish.

Bearing in mind the need to cultivate the above four psychological assets, let's now start moving toward the ways to build grit. The first step toward build grit is to consciously choose a mindset conducive to building grit- and that is called 'growth mindset'

Grit Emanates from Growth Mindset

According to research from Stanford University, by researcher Carol Dweck, grit emanates from a concept called growth mindset. The concept of growth mindset is based the neuroscientific research, which proves the existence of neuroplasticity. Neuroplasticity is an umbrella term referring to the ability of your brain to reorganize itself, both physically and functionally, throughout your life due to your environment, behavior, thinking, and emotions.

As per Dweck's research, the growth mindset is based on the belief that your ability to learn is not set in stone. The people who choose to have a growth mindset are more resilient and tend to push through struggle because they believe that hard work is part of the process and they do not believe that failure is a permanent condition. In a growth mindset, people understand that their talents and abilities can be developed through effort, good teaching, and persistence.

The opposite of a growth mindset is a fixed mindset. Children with a fixed mindset believe they have a certain amount of brains and talent and nothing can change that. People with a fixed mindset tend to believe that effort is a bad thing, if they have what it takes to be smart, gifted or talented by nature than they should not need much effort. This type of belief decreases the motivation to work toward long-term goals.

Interestingly, according to Dweck, simply knowing about the dual concept of growth mindset vs. fixed mindset causes changes in people's belief systems. They are more likely to accept a growth mindset—or the belief that effort, embracing challenges, and seeking out learning opportunities is a stronger predictor of success. This encourages a grittier perspective, contributing to, and wanting to put more effort and time in.

Growth Mindset and Grit Activate Brain Areas Responsible For Achieving Goals

Neuroscience has gone much advanced with the advent of fMRI (functional magnetic resonance imaging) technique, where scientists examine the physical properties and movements within human brain to ascertain the impact of any outside stimuli or internal thinking process.

One 2016 study[7] utilized resting-state fMRI to examine how two important non-cognitive skills, grit, and growth mindset, are associated with *cortico-striatal networks* **important for learning**.

[7]https://www.ncbi.nlm.nih.gov/pmc/articles/PMC50409
06/

Please note that Corticostriatal connections play a central role in developing appropriate **goal-directed behaviors, including the motivation and cognition to develop appropriate actions to obtain a specific outcome**.

In the study, whole-brain seed-to-voxel connectivity was examined for dorsal and ventral striatal seeds. While both grit and growth mindset were associated with functional connectivity between ventral striatal and bilateral prefrontal networks thought to be important for cognitive-behavioral control. There were also clear dissociations between the neural correlates of the two constructs.

Grit, the long-term perseverance toward a goal or set of goals, was associated with ventral striatal networks including connectivity to regions such as the medial prefrontal and rostral anterior cingulate cortices **implicated in perseverance, delay in receipt of reward**. Growth mindset, the belief that effort can improve talents, notably intelligence, was associated with both ventral and dorsal striatal connectivity **with regions thought to be**

important for error-monitoring, such as dorsal anterior cingulate cortex.

Above findings help construct neuro-cognitive models of these non-cognitive skills and have critical implications for character education. Such education is a key component of social and emotional learning, ensuring that children can rise to challenges in the classroom and in life.

Growth mindset is different from your IQ

Now, please understand that growth mindset is different from IQ. IQ says your intelligence is set in stone and you really only have a range to work with. Growth mindset, on the other hand, states that your ability to learn isn't fixed. You can polish it. You can work on it. It is based on your effort. In other words, you can choose to learn. It means your ability to comprehend may be fixed or limited by your IQ, but this doesn't prevent you from trying to learn. You can put in a lot of effort to break down new information in such a way that you can digest it.

Let's put it this way, pretend you could only digest three things at a time. That's all you can do. However, you really like this item, but it's made of six elements. So how do you ingest the six items? You can break it apart. While it's true that you're stuck with three, that's all you can process at one time, there's nothing stopping you from taking six and breaking it down into two sets of threes or three sets of twos. That's how you ingest it. This takes effort. This takes choice.

And the best part to the growth mindset research coming out of Stanford University is that they have shown that physical connections in the brain are actually triggered by what we choose to learn. So if you're a person who really puts in a lot of effort at learning, your brain creates more neural connections. The more memories you have, the more connections are made. The more you think, the more neural connections are formed in your brain.

According to Stanford researchers, when kids are taught that their brains grow and change in response to challenges, these kids are more likely to hang on. They're more likely to persevere. They assume that their ability to learn is not a foregone conclusion, so they're more likely to keep trying. They are taught that failure is not a permanent condition – meaning that it's OK to fail. It's even OK to try only for things not to work out.

Unfortunately, this is the outer limits of where we are in the formal study of grit. Regardless, this book teaches you those elements of growth mindset that are necessary for you to build grit.

Also, it is important to remember that, the growth mindset has two central pillars: (1) the brain grows and changes in response to challenges and information. So the more you challenge it with information, the more it changes. And (2) failure is not a permanent condition; it is just a temporary setback.

Steps to Building Personal Grit

Now, with the above background of growth mindset and its two central pillars, you will learn the important steps in building your personal grit.

Step #1: Belief: The Powerful Tool To Build Grit

Step #2: Strengthen Your Belief Muscles

Step #3: Incorporate your big picture goals into your identity

Step #4: Train yourself to get back on track

Step #5: Create self-sustaining coping mechanisms that keep you focused

Step #6: Adopt best practices that maximize your grit

See you in Chapter 4.

Chapter 4: 5 Toxic Mindsets that Kill Grit

****

"Compared with what we ought to be, we are only half awake. Our fires are damped, our drafts are checked. We are making use of only a small part of our possible mental resources."

– William James

Before we get into the process to building grit, please understand there are certain mindsets that will destroy your ability to build grit. That's right, you're not even going to make much progress developing this trait unless you get rid of unwanted mindsets.

These mindsets undermine your ability to focus. They also lead you to waste precious mental and emotional resources that you could otherwise devote to building grit.

Toxic Mindset #1: Sense of Entitlement

When people feel life has to be fair or that they have to start any kind of project at the top, they have a sense of entitlement. And let me tell you, this is the most toxic attitude and mindset you could ever adopt, because nothing's going to happen.

Life has always been unfair. That's always been the case. And people who have been successful had to deal with this reality. They did not wish it away, they did not waste precious time trying to make things "right." Instead, they chose to deal with reality the way it exists instead of the way they wish it existed.

So instead of focusing on how things should be, focus on how things are and keep your eyes on the prize. Otherwise, it's very easy for you to feel like a victim.

There are two types of people in life. There are victims, and there are victors. Victims sit around asking what happened. Victors, on the other hand, make things happen. This doesn't change the fact that life will always remain unfair. The only question that begs to be asked is, what are you going to do about it?

So please understand you are not entitled to respect. Respect has to be earned. You're not entitled to victory. Victory is paid for by pain, sacrifice, and often times, betrayal. That's just the way life is. The sooner you understand how life works, the sooner you will be able to step up and deal with it accordingly. Otherwise, you will continue to get beaten down again and again until your will is broken.

The vast majority of people are born with tremendous potential. We all have the potential to be the next Bill Gates, Warren Buffett, or Elon Musk, but most of us never choose to go that route. We either let ourselves get defeated by the disconnect between how we think things should be and how they really are. When you consistently do that, you're only making things harder on yourself.

Toxic Mindset #2: Short-term Mindset

People with this type of mindset believe that they need to get rich quickly. They believe that the moment they put in some sort of effort, they are entitled to instant results.

Short-term mindsets have destroyed otherwise brilliant people throughout history. These people have the potential to really change the world for the better. They have the IQ, they have the emotional quotient, they have the social skills, but the problem is, their time horizon is so short that they're always looking for the instant payout.

And when this doesn't happen, they lose heart. They become discouraged, and they play all sorts of mental games with themselves. They either convince themselves that the goal simply was not worth it to begin with, or the rich are getting richer and the poor are getting poorer. In other words, they come up with all sorts of justifications and excuses that deflect their focus away from the real problem.

The issue is not whether the goal is worthy. The problem is that your expectations of return are just so unrealistic that you're just defeating yourself by sucking out your motivation. If you believe that the payoffs have to be instant or have to happen soon enough, you're not going to develop grit. In fact, this is the precise opposite of grit. Grit means sticking to the plan regardless of how long it takes. Grit involves sticking with a process despite the fact that the reward is nowhere in sight.

You're running a marathon. Unfortunately, people with short-term mindsets have convinced themselves that life is essentially a giant sprint. They acknowledge that long-term results and success require long timelines, but this is just an intellectual acceptance at surface level. In terms of real belief, they're stuck with instant payouts.

This really is a shame because a lot of very talented and otherwise gifted people suffer from short-term mindsets. And this short circuits whatever potential they may have.

Toxic Mindset #3: Others Are To Blame for What's Wrong In Your Life

It's really important to make sure that before you work to build your personal grit you stop blaming other people for what's wrong with your life.

As I've mentioned earlier, when you blame others for your frustrations, you are essentially handing them control over your life. Seriously. Because if you're convinced that another person caused all your problems, then it logically follows that they also have the solution. After all, they created the damage, they must have the answers. The moment this assignment happens, you are essentially abdicating all power to change your personal reality. In other words, you have given up responsibility for your life.

This is a serious problem, because you can't control those people. They have their own lives to live. In fact, in many cases, they don't even remember the harm they did you. But here you are, constantly looking for others to blame; constantly looking in the past for trauma that happened a long time ago to explain why you're so frustrated in the present.

You have to understand that until and unless there is some sort of time machine in the future, the past is the past. There's really nothing we could do to change it. The best thing you can do is to stop blaming others and stop looking at your past as a ready source of excuses for why you shouldn't try as hard as you should in the present time.

Toxic Mindset #4: Constantly Comparing Yourself to Others

What if I told you that even the most successful and powerful people in the world can easily make themselves feel miserable? If you don't believe me, imagine Mark Zuckerberg, the billionaire inventor and founder of Facebook, comparing himself to Michael Jordan in terms of basketball abilities.

Zuckerberg may be a multi-billionaire, but I'm sure he sucks on the hard court. Michael Jordan, on the other hand, is a legend. There is no comparison. But the problem is, if Mark Zuckerberg compares himself to Michael Jordan, he will come out a loser. Imagine that, a multi-billionaire who shapes political realities through the power of Facebook feeling lousy, feeling small, feeling insignificant. That's right, feeling like a total failure.

I bring up this imaginary comparison to bring home the point that if you want to make yourself feel miserable, you only need to compare yourself to others. This works all the time. What you do is you compare something that you don't have to the very best that somebody else has. It's like a fish comparing itself to a lion in terms of the ability to walk. Does that make any sense? Well, if it doesn't, then you should stop doing it.

And unfortunately, if you're looking to build grit and you have the mental habit of constantly comparing yourself to others, you will destroy your ability to build grit. It's just simply not going to happen. You will always allow yourself to be held back by imagined insecurities and inadequacies. And what's even worse is that the more you focus on the things that you're missing, the weaker, smaller, and less significant you feel. This works like a charm. It's like some sort of mental and emotional quicksand.

You have to understand that other people in this world would love to be in your shoes. You may be thinking to yourself, "I don't have that much money." Well, what if I told you that hundreds of millions of people on planet earth live on less than $2 a day?

So count your blessings. Stop comparing yourself to others and focus on what you should be focusing on, which should be your big goals in life.

Toxic Mindset #5: Belief in Final States – Assuming Things as Permanent

People who have this mindset believe that if you experience any kind of reality, it is absolute and it never ends. For example, you work on a project and, for a variety of reasons, it failed. Maybe the company ran out of money, strategic people left – whatever the reason, the project fell apart.

You may look at the situation and think that this setback is permanent; that it cannot be turned around. You look at the project parameters and you conclude that regardless of who handles it and regardless of the circumstances surrounding it, it will always end in failure. This is a classic example of a final state mindset.

What if I told you that oftentimes, it takes only one small change in variables for a project to turn out completely different? What if I told you that successful companies like Facebook and Google only had to have one parameter changed in their corporate evolution and history for them to flat out fail?

Similarly, this can also work in reverse. You can look at a company that failed, for example, Kodak Eastman, the previously huge camera and film company. If the evolution of digital cameras only took a different path, Kodak Eastman might still be a big company. It might still be around.

The problem with people with final state mindsets is they assume life only goes in one direction. They believe that everything is predestined because things worked out that way. What if I told you that the chaos theory of life is always in effect?

Chaos theory states that when you look at any complex process, it only takes one small change in a variable to replicate that effect throughout the system and, at the end of the day, because of the exponential change in direction, things turn out very differently. Weather patterns are a good example of this.

Life is a series of variables, and just because things turned out a certain way, it doesn't necessarily mean that it will always take that direction. We have to look at the different variables at play and, most importantly, always remember that we are in control of our lives. So when these variables come into play, we can make better decisions. We can make better choices, and this can mean all the difference in the world as far as the success and failure of our projects are concerned.

When you believe in final states, you are simply undermining yourself. You are saying to yourself you really have no control over your life. You are saying to yourself that whatever decision you make doesn't matter because everything is already predestined. Everything is already set in stone. Talk about disempowering. You're basically denying yourself the ability to author your life.

Therefore, you've got to keep the above 5 toxic mindsets in mind before you work on building your grit. Most importantly, study them very closely and see if they apply to you. Do yourself a big favor and seek to neutralize these or overcome them. Otherwise, you're not going to build the grit that you need to achieve the success that you are otherwise capable of achieving.

It doesn't matter whether you want to be a superstar at school or you want to reach the highest heights in the corporate world. It doesn't matter whether you want to be some sort of athletic superstar or a musical genius. All of these require grit because victory is never handed to you. You have to fight for it. You have to negotiate for it.

If it isn't possible through the front door, you have to try the side door. If that is off limits, you have to dig a basement. If you can't do that, you have to hit it from the back. If that won't work, then you go through the ceiling. Whatever the case may be, you never take no for an answer. That is the key to grit. Remember the words of Martin Luther King Jr., when he said:

"If you can't fly, then run. If you can't run, then walk. If you can't walk, then crawl. but whatever you do, you have to keep moving"

Unfortunately, these 5 toxic mindsets kill your ability to develop grit. Neutralize these before you start your project, otherwise, you'll be wasting your time.

Now let's move on to learn the steps to building grit.

Chapter 5: Energize the Power of Belief

"One person with a belief is equal to a force of ninety-nine who have only interest."

~ John Stewart Mill

The first step in building grit, as guided by the growth mindset approach involves the power of belief. Belief is crucial to building grit. If you don't believe in the right things, it's going to be almost impossible for you to hang on to your big goals in life.

It would be very hard for you to focus on the big picture because ultimately, you don't believe you will be able to achieve it. Somehow, some way, you believe you don't have what it takes to go all the way. You have to understand that your ability to control what you choose to believe in impacts grit. Belief, just like grit, is a choice. You can choose to believe in certain things and choose to be skeptical about other things.

A lot of people are under the impression that if they grow up with parents who believe in certain things that somehow, some way, their parent's beliefs get passed on to them. This is not true. There's no such thing as belief by osmosis. You can't just passively absorb your previous generation's beliefs. Instead, this is all a choice. You can choose whether to believe what your parents believe. Not just about God, but about everything else in life. You can choose your values. These are not handed to you by your parents with no choice on your part. It is always a choice.

It's important to keep this in mind because a lot of people are under the impression that somehow, belief can be passively absorbed. This is not true. Because if you truly believe that, then you really don't have any control over your life. You are essentially a meat puppet because somebody you do not control can somehow beam these beliefs to you and you just passively accept it with no control over the process.

It doesn't work that way. You can be quite passive about it and just sit back and let everything in, but even doing that is a choice made by you. There is always an element of choice there. You would decide.

What is Belief?

Belief is the mental acceptance that certain things are facts. Belief is the state of mind in which a person thinks something to be the case with or without there being experimental evidence to prove that something is the case with factual certainty.

Simply, a belief defines an idea or principle which we judge to be true. Belief is just our judgment about a particular thing or person. For example, you may believe that a person is arrogant, simply because he or she doesn't talk much, whereas the factual position could be that the person might be an introverted one. But you continue to believe in your idea, until it's proven false. That's the way belief system works.

One of the world's best-known skeptics and critical thinkers, Michael Shermer, also the author of *The Believing Brain: From Spiritual Faiths to Political Convictions – How We Construct Beliefs and Reinforce Them as Truths* has explored into the reasoning of why people believe anything at all. The summary of his thesis is straightforward, as he states below:

"**We form our beliefs** for a variety of subjective, personal, emotional, and psychological reasons in the context of environments created by family, friends, colleagues, culture, and society at large; **after forming our beliefs we then defend, justify, and rationalize them** with a host of intellectual reasons, cogent arguments, and rational explanations. Beliefs come first, explanations for beliefs follow."

Take another example, if you come to know the man who calls himself your father is not your biological father, but is actually a stepfather, this is going to change how you view that person. Similarly, whatever facts that may be revealed about your biological father, it may have certain predictive values as far as your health is concerned. It may even go a long way to explain why you behave the way you do or you have certain habits.

Do you see how this works? And it's interesting to see the change in people's attitudes before and after they learned certain facts.

Make no mistake about it, when you accept certain things as true, they change your conception of who you are and how you respond to certain situations as well as your perception of your capabilities. In fact, belief can lead to self-fulfilling prophecies and predictions. This happens because when you believe in certain things long enough, it changes your assumptions.

Belief Doesn't Always Mean Truth

Prior to May 6th, 1954, it was a common belief among athletes that humans couldn't run a mile in 4 minutes. The general consensus around the world was that it was physically impossible. Even experts believed that human body was just not capable of it. Now this belief rang true for ages. But on May 6th, 1954, Roger Bannister ran the miracle mile in 3:59:4, to be exact—becoming the first man ever to do so, breaking through the mystical barrier. By doing this, he didn't only break a world record, but he broke a limiting belief in the minds of hundreds of athletes. With that one crossing a mile in under 4 minutes, the power of belief showed. Thereafter, athletes trained and had a new achievable goal, and more began to break the 4-minute mark.

You see, if Bannister had believed in that false assumption of human limitation, he'd have already quit, even before trying. That's the power of belief.

Therefore, don't for a second think your choice of belief doesn't have a major impact. In fact, your life's direction can change dramatically based on what you choose to believe regarding who you are, what you're capable of, where you came from, and other serious issues.

Belief Makes Legends

Have you heard the real-life story of Albert Einstein, the great scientist, famously known as the father of modern physics, which exemplifies the power of belief?

Einstein was slow in learning how to speak. His mother was summoned to the school by Einstein's school authorities. The school headmaster told her child had below average intelligence and issued a note to that effect stating he could not study in the school. The headmaster even expressed his view to her that Einstein would not amount to much in his life.

His mother kept that note from the school hidden in an iron box and also tightly as a secret in her heart too, till her last breath. She told Einstein he was a super intelligent child, in fact, a genius and therefore, he couldn't study with other normal kids. Einstein believed in his mother's statement and did the amazing stuff in the field of physics, leading to winning a coveted Nobel Prize in Physics.

In the later years, when his mother died, Einstein stumbled across that old iron box kept by his mother and out of curiosity, he opened it. He was utterly shocked after seeing that note from school and couldn't stop crying, as he realized his mother had done the best thing possible by not showing him that letter.

He was amazed to know the power of belief—the belief his mother had installed in his mind that he was a genius. Had his mother told him the truth about the reason for being expelled from the school, probably he wouldn't ever have reached such greater heights in his life.

You see the point. Belief can even generate geniuses, so don't think what you choose to believe and not believe doesn't have an impact on your life. It has a tremendous impact because it leads to self-fulfilling prophecies.

The good news? Belief is a choice. You can always choose to accept other things as facts. You always have a choice. You can choose what facts to believe and, most importantly, what they mean.

What Do You Need to Believe?

When you're working to build grit, what do you need to believe? Well, you need to **believe in the big goal you've set for yourself**. You have to accept certain key elements as facts and choose what it is and you have to define what it's not.

You also have to believe that it is **worth pursuing** this goal. Because without this choice, it's going to be hard for you to build grit because you're chasing a ghost. You're basically thinking, "It would be nice if that thing happened, but it's not big enough for me. It isn't worthy enough".

The next thing you need to believe is that **it's doable**. In other words, as big and as intimidating as this big goal may be, it is still doable. You can convert it from an idea or concept to something that you can see, hear, touch, taste, and smell. It can be reduced to reality.

Sounds good so far, right? Well, the problem is, even if you go through all these steps, you may still not believe enough for your big goal to become a reality. You may still not believe enough to be successful. There's one more step missing: **you have**

to believe you can achieve the big goal.

Let me tell you, believing in a big goal that other people can achieve is easy. You're basically just kicking the ball to other people. That doesn't really help you. For you to develop grit to achieve your big goals in life, you have to believe *you* can achieve those big goals, not other people. They may be able to do it, but what matters is whether you believe you can do it.

This is crucial because a lot of people allow themselves to think in terms of limitations. Either they say to themselves that they're not smart enough, they weren't born into a rich family, there are too many people competing against them, they're not good looking enough, and a long laundry list of excuses. This is a very important step because when you choose to truly believe you can do this big goal, you get rid of that list.

Belief Just Doesn't Remain Mental – It Impacts Everything

A lot of critics are under the impression that belief is just something that you play in your mind; that it's some sort of mind game. It isn't. Because you have to understand that when you choose to believe in certain things and you turn your back on believing in other things, your assumptions change. Once this happens, your emotional responses to certain things in life change.

If you believe a goal is worthwhile, then you're no longer going to respond to fatigue and frustration the same way you used to respond to them before you adopted that goal. Do you see how this works? It's like you're flipping a switch. You start talking about different things now with this new belief. You also start changing how you deal with setbacks. Most importantly, when you believe in certain goals, it changes your actions. Your behavior becomes different. This all leads to hope.

When you believe your goal is achievable, it gives you hope. It gives you something to focus on and something to plan for. It gives what you do today, in the here and now, meaning and purpose.

You're not just spinning your wheels. You're not just waiting for one day to flow into another with no consequence. Instead, you measure the days to when you will be able to eventually achieve that grand goal you have set for yourself.

What's the best part to all of this? Well, actually, **belief gets the ball rolling** because you create a self-sustaining process as you work toward your big dreams. It works like this. When you choose to believe, you create hope. And when you start taking action on your hopes, you create even more hope, you take more action, and your beliefs get strengthened, and on and on it goes. It's **an upward spiral**.

And it all starts with a choice of believing in a certain way. Let's move on to the next chapter now.

Chapter 6: Strengthen & Rewire Your Belief System

"A belief is not merely an idea the mind possesses; it is an idea that possesses the mind."

~Robert Bolton

As I have mentioned in a previous chapter, intellectually accepting something on the surface is not enough. Things may fall into place in your mind, but until you change your behavior because of what you choose to believe, nothing will change.

Belief, just by itself, isn't going to change your life. It must impact your actions.

The stories on the power of belief in the previous chapter highlight that once you deeply imbibe a belief, the fact you believed something as true, triggers you to take the different types of actions, and those actions have the power to change your life.

Again to emphasize the truth, belief by itself will lead to nothing if it just stays in your head. Intellectual level belief doesn't do much. You need a level of emotional urgency, which pushes you to change your actions. When you truly believe in something, it starts a chain reaction because it never operates in a vacuum. One question is usually tied to other issues.

Your belief becomes reality. It has an outward manifestation because now, people have something that they can detect. It is not just happening in your mind. You're not just kicking around ideas. You're no longer in the world of theory.

The harsh reality is the world doesn't care about your feelings. Once you take action, then only then will the world take notice. The world is objective—it only pays attention to results. It couldn't care less what you think you could have done, should have done, or would have done. It doesn't care about your regrets, guilt, or remorse, unless these change your actions. The world is all about action.

Belief Grows When You Practice It

How do you grow your belief? How do you engage your power of belief? It all boils down to allowing yourself to be challenged. Put yourself in the position where your belief is called into question.

For example, if you believe you're a good swimmer, put yourself in a situation where people can question your swimming abilities. Usually, this takes the form of competition. At that point, you really have only two choices. You can start believing their negative impressions of your skills as a swimmer, or you can choose to believe you're a good swimmer. If you choose to continue to believe in your abilities, then this means that you're going to continue to practice, you're going to continue to compete, and you're going to try to prove them wrong. This strengthens your belief because you focus your actions on achieving results that would support what you choose to believe about yourself.

But guess what? It only takes one yes for your belief about you to be strengthened and reinforced. It only takes one yes for you to get the energy and the faith you need to try again and again. You have to put yourself in a position where your belief is called into question and you choose to continue believing.

Believe me, there is nothing fun about being rejected, but if you believe that you have something positive to contribute to an organization, then you would go on one job interview after another. You would continue to take rejection after rejection, but it wouldn't matter. You truly believe that you have something to offer, so you go on one job interview after another until you land that job. That's the power of faith.

Your belief grows when you take action on it. It doesn't always lead to a happy result. Often times, you get hit with a rejection, and they come in waves. But the more you put yourself in a position to challenge your belief, the stronger it will become with each victory. The more you act out of faith, the stronger your faith and hope become.

The key here is action. This is not just an emotional state of you believing something is really true, but it just stays in your head. You just get a nice emotional rush. Trust me, that's worthless. That's not going to do anything for you. It's not going to change your life. You may imagine that you're the best employee ever, but until and unless you go to that interview, nothing's going to happen.

Strengthen Your Secondary Beliefs

Building grit means focusing on the big picture. This big picture may become a reality in a few months, in a few years, or maybe after a few decades—you're in for a long ride. Therefore, to take sustainable action for that long trail, you have to make sure that your belief system is a 'system' indeed.

What is a system? It is a set of items that are arranged in a certain way and work in a pre-determined fashion. They form part of a process where something happens for another thing to take place. These different parts have to work together to create a flow. If a single part of the system doesn't work properly, it can't remain dysfunctional in isolation, rather it affects the entire chain of activities in that system.

For your beliefs, you also have to have an entire belief system. You can't just believe in one big belief. You can't just believe in your big goal because if you pick it apart, there are other smaller related beliefs that hold up or lead to the big goal. In other words, there's a complex of beliefs that need to be in place. These are your secondary beliefs, which support your main and big belief.

How does this work? What exactly do you need to believe for your big goal to happen?

Let's break this up to understand it well. What should be your biggest belief? The growth mindset outlook warrants that **you should believe you have the ability to achieve it**. This is a big one because this means you're not going to be relying on other people. You're not going to allow yourself to think that being part of a group will enable you to achieve your goal. No. You have to believe that you, yourself, individually, would be able to achieve your big goal. Though, your group might help in terms of inspiration. They might be able to connect you with the right people to open doors from time to time, but ultimately, it's only your belief that can do it, will move the needle, no other person can achieve your goal for you.

Now coming to secondary beliefs, the other web of assumptions you need to believe, as a part of belief system, is **the faith that you have the skills** to make your big goal happen. You may not have the skills now, but you have to believe that you would be able to acquire them later on, by putting sincere efforts. For example, if your big goal is to launch a massive technology company that would disrupt the internet, you might be looking at technology that doesn't quite exist just yet. The skill sets are not present yet, but you believe that you will be able to acquire them in the future. Regardless, this is a key part of that web of assumptions. You have to believe that you have the skills or can get the skills.

The same applies to having the **right resources**. Either they are present now, or you can get them when you need them.

Regardless, you need to make sure you will have the resources when they are needed so you can realize your big goals.

Finally, you also have to **believe that your resources, skills, contacts, social networks, and everything else will line up** with circumstances as they present themselves. These are big assumptions to make and you need to believe these. Otherwise, you might end up sabotaging yourself.

You have to look at your big goal as something that's framed within a larger context and all those other items need your attention. You have to believe that they are there. You have to devote enough mental energy so they get your focus. By paying attention to these details, you would be able to take action in a systematic and methodical way so that everything is lined up properly. This means that the right things happen at the right time to produce the right results with the right people.

It's a system. You can't look at your big goal as some sort of one-shot big shot affair. It's not like you're Luke Skywalker in an X-wing fighter shooting for that big hole in the Death Star where you only need to sink that shot and the Death Star will blow up. Well, to reach that point in the Star Wars saga, a lot of things had to happen before that. The rebels had to know exactly where the weak spot was. They have to map out the defenses of the Death Star.

Unfortunately, if you are laboring under the one-shot big shot delusion, it's easy to think that you just need to show up at the right place at the right time, do the right thing, and everything will fall into place. Its' not going to happen that way. You have to plan ahead. In other words, you have to take care of the web of assumptions that hold up your big goal. You need to make sure that the conditions they set are met.

If you want to have a realistic shot, then you have to believe in the right things. There has to be a web of beliefs, which turns into assumptions that hold up and make your big goal possible.

Expect Your Belief to Get Rocked

Consistently acting on belief, means you're consistently running the risk of failing. And this is good news. As I've mentioned above, if you practice your belief and you act out of faith, your belief grows. It gets stronger and stronger. It's kind of like getting a scar on your skin. The first time you get scratched, it's going to hurt. The skin will be very tender. But as it heals and then gets scratched again, the inconvenience lessens over time. Eventually, your skin gets used to it. It would take a really deep gash for you to even feel it.

Similarly, we develop mental scar tissue as well. Things that knocked us off track in the past doesn't even faze us now. You might get that rejection that is going to be so crushing, so demoralizing and so painful that you stand back and ask yourself, "What am I doing?" Get ready for that.

Let me tell you, the induction period or the wind-up period where you get used to strengthening your belief and acting on it can be rough. Remember, just like anything else in life, the first time you try something is the hardest time. You don't know what to expect, you don't know how to act, it's easy to blow things out of proportion, but this is precisely what you should expect. **Robin Sharma** once rightly said:

> *"Every   Change is hard   at   the beginning, messy   in the   middle and gorgeous at the end."*

Therefore, expect to get rocked. Expect the pain. Expect the loss. Just keep pushing forward. Get past that induction period, but this varies from person to person.

Some people fall into place the first time they get rejected. They're able to figure things out, they connect the dots, and things proceed fairly smoothly after that point. Others take a while. Personally, I'm the type of person who needs to get knocked back several times before I get the memo. Regardless, you have to survive through the induction period.

The good news is, the more victories you rack up, the easier it gets because your belief is slowly being baked into your lived experience. You no longer feel that you are acting out of hope of things that you really can't see. Instead, you've seen how your belief paid off in the past.

This has happened regularly enough so you no longer feel like you're acting out of hope that things will fall into place. At the back of your head, you know that you've done this before and chances are quite good, you're going to do it again this time around.

Unfortunately, there is no fixed timeline that applies to everybody. Some people get to this stage sooner than others. Others take a long, long time. What is true, however, is that you need to get to this stage.

OK, now let's move on to the next section.

Chapter 7: Incorporate Your Big Goals into Your Identity

****

"Only one who devotes himself to a cause with his whole strength and soul can be a true master. For this reason mastery demands all of a person."

~ Albert Einstein

Please understand if you have a big vision or plan for your life, it's very hard for you to consistently work toward it if it's all floating out there. If you think your big ambition in life is just something that's outside of you, or something that would be nice to see happen, it's anybody's guess whether you'd actually achieve it. Even if you follow the previous steps you learned so far, you're still going to fall short.

You have to be so emotionally invested in your big picture goal or your big goals that they become part of who you are. If it's something you can easily turn your back on or easily leave on the table, then chances are, there will be other more pressing stuff to take care of. That's just how the human mind works.

Your Big Picture Goal Cannot Remain Outside of You

When somebody is wishing, dreaming, and hoping, this person is basically engaging in a mental exercise. They're thinking of their life now and what it could be like in the future. They're thinking of possibilities and what changes they would like.

This is all important, but something's missing. It isn't personal enough yet. The stakes are not high enough because if you can think of alternate realities, you're essentially just watching a movie in reverse.

When you watch a movie, you suspend your disbelief and you allow the creator of that movie to feed your mind with an alternative reality. You sit back for a couple of hours, enjoy yourself, and then go on with the rest of your life. When you're wishing, hoping and dreaming, you're doing the same thing.

But instead of somebody giving you some sort of canned entertainment, you provide the script yourself. You provide the visuals. You provide the movie. But it's still a movie.

At some point, you're going to get up, stop the movie, and go on with the rest of your life. Later on, you will play another movie, then another movie after that. This is how wishes, dreams, and hopes play out.

Now, don't get me wrong, they are personal to a certain extent. They do make you feel really good. For example, if you're unemployed right now and you're struggling to pay the rent, it would be great if you could sit back and daydream about becoming a millionaire. Wouldn't it be awesome to have loads of money in your bank account? Wouldn't it be great to drive around in your dream car?

When you engage in this visualization, however, the main benefit is you're getting a temporary relief from the harsh reality you are living out right now. But the problem is you're not planning on working toward achieving your goals. Rather, you're just playing a mental movie that transports you from having to deal with the reality facing you. But you've to be cautious here—you're not building grit when you do this. Instead, you are anesthetizing yourself from taking action. The more you daydream, the less likely it would be for you to actually act on a plan.

I hope this is clear because there's a big difference between just wishing, hoping and dreaming instead of buckling up and planning to make your goals and vision come true. Because **grit requires action**.

Your personal goals and vision must be part of who you are. They need to be deeply ingrained in your identity. This requires you to take ownership of your big picture or ultimate goal. There has to be some sort of do or die component. You have to give all of you and become one with your goal. Read below quote by Henry Rollins, which aptly sums up what you need to do:

"If you have an idea of what you want to do in your future, you must go at it with almost monastic obsession, be it music, the ballet or just a basic degree. You have to go at it single-

mindedly and let nothing get in your way."

– Henry Rollins

You have to identify your deeper personal identity – You have to know and claim who you are. Because, as someone rightly said once: *"Your identity precedes your activity."*

You have to say to yourself, "This is my destiny. This is who I am. This is my personality and the type of person I was born to be." When you do that, you visualize your big picture goal. It becomes part of your daily routine.

And you're not just doing this to get some sort of emotional escape from the things that you have to deal with. You don't play this mental picture of you sitting in a corner office of a big corporate to transport you from your misery of being unemployed. Instead, you look at this alternate reality as the end goal of all your current actions.

Compare this to being unemployed and thinking of yourself as a senior corporate employee and allowing yourself to be pumped up by that vision to start sending out a lot more resumes. You can also use that vision to motivate you to rewrite your resume so it's more compelling. You may get so pumped up that you change your personal references to get better ones.

Whatever the case may be, this is a far cry from daydreaming because when you're daydreaming, you just get the emotional rush and nothing else. It's kind of like a mental sugar high. It's like eating empty calories. You get amped up for a few minutes and then you crash, so you "take another hit" and you visualize again to get a nice emotional high, then you repeat this, but you don't end up doing anything.

When your big picture goals become part of your identity—your thoughts, emotions, daily talk, and actions flow toward it. It's not just something you picture in your mind to give you a nice emotional rush.

People engage in **self-talk**. This doesn't mean they are actually talking to themselves. You don't hear anything. But mentally, they're playing a script. Your big picture goal must be part of that script.

Don't think this self-talk is a woo-woo or mystical thing to do. Rather sport's psychology research[8] confirms the positive effect of self-talk on performance. Sportsmen usually keep on doing positive self-talk to improve their technique and focus, and you can use self-talk to improve your performance outside of sports as well. You can use it to improve your focus on the task at hand or to motivate yourself when you're going through adverse times. Positive self-talk can provide you with a short-term boost of motivation.

You should also **keep a journal**. And in your journal, you should always talk about your big picture goal. You have to remain engaged.

Finally, you should create **daily physical reminders** of your big picture goal. For example, if you want to get into Harvard Law School, you should have the Harvard

---

[8]

https://www.tandfonline.com/doi/abs/10.1080/104132
00701230613

Law logo or pictures of the Harvard Law School buildings on your PC. Whatever the case may be, as you go about your day, you are constantly physically and visually reminded of your big goal.

That's how you know you have fully internalized it. It's not just something that you take out when you need to feel good or when you need to escape your daily hassles. That is not your big picture goal. That is an escape—simply a cop-out. You can't allow yourself to fall into the rabbit hole of escapism. That leads nowhere. Instead, when you visualize your big picture goals, it must be part of a larger series or a system of practices that make that big picture goal a more immediate part of your personal reality and identity.

Recruit Others into Your Big Goal

As the old saying goes, two heads are better than one. This is especially true when it comes to people working toward a goal. When two people believe in the same thing, they keep talking about it and inspiring each other to action and reporting their progress. They then get closer and closer to their goals.

When you work your way to your goal, there are going to be setbacks. There are going to be rough spots. There are going to be bumps along the road. It would be great to have somebody you're traveling with to hold you up, encourage you, and inspire you when things fall apart.

You have to recruit others into your big goal. It doesn't have to be complicated. You don't have to sign a contract with each other, you don't have to have fully defined roles. Simply telling others about your goal can help you tremendously.

Believe it or not, if you have a big goal like losing weight for example, and you post it on your Facebook page, you'd be surprised as to how motivated you become. Let's face it, a lot of people are not very proactive. They know they should lose weight, they know they should look for a better job, they know that they should be better parents. Whatever the case may be, they cannot motivate themselves around the things that they should be doing. They know these things are important, but they feel that they have other more pressing stuff to do.

Now, the moment they post their goal on Facebook, there is the risk of social shame. In that instance, people then start becoming reactive. In other words, you may not be the type of person who gets motivated by the things you should be doing or by focusing on how you stand to gain, but you may be motivated by fear. You may be motivated by focusing on things you stand to lose. When you post your goal on Facebook, you stand to lose your reputation. You say to everybody, "I'm going to lose 30 pounds six months from now," and you enter a date.

Now, it may well turn out that people didn't even see your post or couldn't care less, but it matters to you because at the back of your mind, there is a risk that somebody would actually call you out on it. This might just be what you need to get going. The remote risk of social shame may be the spark that you need to get your act together. You have to recruit others into your big goal and public declarations can definitely do it.

Another approach you can take is to allow your closest friends to hold you accountable. These involve your best friends, these are people who you truly respect, or maybe they are close relatives.

First, you tell them your goals and you give them full permission to make you feel bad if you don't pursue those goals. If you fall behind or if you start to slack off or if you start forgetting about your goals, they have full permission to call you out. They have full permission to scold you. They have full permission to nag you. You have to be clear about the permission you're giving them.

The great thing about allowing your closest friends or your relatives to hold you to account is the fact that they love you. When you love somebody, even if you don't really care about the stuff they like, you start liking that stuff because you love them. That's how close personal bonds work. Things that matter to your loved ones start mattering to you because you love them.

Use this to your advantage. Allow your closest friends to hold you to account. They may be very pudgy and couldn't care less about losing weight, but since they see that it's important to you, they'll get into it as well. They'll hold you to account because they know it means so much to you. Since they love you, they would hold you to account.

The Key

The key here is actually quite simple. By keeping your goal in mind, it becomes very hard to let go. It becomes part of your identity. You start living, eating, sleeping, drinking and thinking about your goal in so many ways every single moment. When you arrange things this way, it gets harder and harder for you to get off track. It becomes the overarching soundtrack of your life. It becomes the **GPS system of your life**.

It's always there. You may be doing something else, but it's always in the background and it's always calling you. It's always directing you. How can it not? It has become part of your identity.

Chapter 8: Effective Ways to Deal With Adversities

****

"Life is not about how fast you run, or how high you climb, but how well you bounce."

~ Vivian Komori

Believe it or not, people with a lot of grit thought about the worst-case scenario and have grown to accept it. They would think about what the worst possible outcome would be as they pursue their big goal. They go through the list of disasters, disappointments and let downs. They sort through all sorts of nightmare scenarios and, at the end of the day, they say, "I'll take it".

They made peace with the possible outcomes. They would say to themselves, "What's the worst-case scenario that could happen? How bad could it be?" And they dream up of all sorts of exaggerated scenarios. But at the end of the day, they decide whatever they stand to gain is much more valuable, precious, and worthwhile than what they stand to lose.

This is crucial. You have to do this as you train your eyes on your big goal.

Earlier in the book, you learned about the web of assumptions you have to have for you to keep working on your big goal. The good news is, the more you believe in these secondary beliefs and more you strengthen these assumptions, the stronger your faith in your big goal becomes. It becomes harder and harder to throw you off. Your resolve gets stronger as you act on these smaller beliefs because when they start producing results and you can see that they pan out, that they are worth believing in, your faith in your big goal gets stronger and stronger.

Sounds awesome, right? But there is one thing that will jeopardize all of this. Unfortunately, it is so easy to do because it's so tempting. What is the worst thing you can do at this stage? Well, you may start assuming that reaching your big goal will be quick and easy. Maybe you started seeing great results and you would assume that since these results are coming in waves, it's only a matter of short time now until you get to your big goal very quickly. You mistake a positive pattern for a quick, easy and painless elevator ride to the top. Regardless of how you come about this mindset, assuming that you will reach your big goal quickly and easily will kill your grit.

It really will because you have to understand that grit is the personal mental and emotional stamina needed to keep hanging on despite the setbacks, disappointments, and pain of your success journey. The hits keep coming, but you keep stepping. You keep moving forward. You may get pushed back, so you move sideways, and then forward. You get slapped around and knocked back, so you get back on your feet and then slide around to try to move forward. If that doesn't work, you try something else. And again and again it goes.

The problem is, if you assume your big goal will now be quick and easy because a lot of things started to pan out and a lot of your secondary beliefs led to easy wins, your grit starts to evaporate. You start developing an **entitlement mentality**, which is a state of mind where you start to believe the privileges endowed upon you are your right. This mental cancer will get the better of you. You have to do yourself a big favor and catch yourself if you start assuming that just because you hit a nice, smooth patch that everything else will proceed smoothly. Because if you believe that, you are really saying to yourself that you deserve a smooth ride.

It'll be disheartening to know, but nobody deserves a pass on the rough road to success. It's narrow and hard for a reason. That's why relatively few people achieve success. Thinking that somehow, since things started to fall into place, that your ultimate victory will come sooner is a mistake. What you're really doing is you're developing an entitlement mentality.

The Reality

You have to get ready for a reality check. The reality is you will get knocked back. It's not a question of if, but when.

You have to be prepared for the rejection. Maybe this will take the form of females rejecting you or laughing at you. Maybe you'll get turned down for a job. Maybe you'll hit a rough patch where you apply to jobs and nobody gives you an offer. Maybe this can take the form of a school where you take test after test and the best you can manage is a C.

These events happen. It's only a matter of time. The issue here is not whether you should avoid it. You can't and you shouldn't. Instead, the issue should be how you are going to deal with it.

Choose to Deal with Setbacks in a Way that Keeps You Focused on the Big Picture

So how exactly do you deal with setbacks that you know will happen?

The first thing you need to do is to be prepared mentally. In other words, you have to believe that yes, setbacks, disappointments, failure, rejection do happen. But they don't have to be permanent. They don't have to rule out your future. You can work around them. You have to deal with setbacks. Assume that it will happen. Don't allow yourself to be surprised. Don't allow yourself to get emotionally drained by the experience.

When it does happen, despite your best efforts at prevention, don't take it lying down. Don't let it hit you like a ton of bricks. Say to yourself, "Well, I tried, and I'm going to keep trying because this happens to the best of us." Say that phrase or say something similar to it. You're not giving an excuse, you're not washing your hands of responsibility, instead you are resolving to keep pushing forward.

Snap into Your Fallback Position

You have to have some sort of fallback position when you get knocked back. In wrestling, when wrestlers get hit—and believe me, a lot of the hits are real, despite the common belief that wrestling is fake; it may well mostly be fake, but a lot of the hits are real—skilled wrestlers don't avoid the hits. Instead, they learn how to take the hit.

In other words, they have a fallback position. So when they get hit, they don't fall flat on their backs. They fall in a certain way or they assume a certain position which allows them to spring back into shape. You should do the same mentally. You should have certain fallback positions when the worst outcome happens.

If you get disappointed or you are dealt a nasty setback, you can choose to do the following:

You can choose to learn. This is always a good idea. Or you can choose to actively find an alternative route. You know that the door ahead of you closed. There are no two ways about it. This is beyond dispute. You say to yourself, "OK, I'm going to move on. I'm going to accept this". But you start looking for an alternative route. This is your personal GPS— your grit kicking in. It tells you in that pleasant voice, "Recalculating route".

Another fallback position **you could take is to change your sub-goals**. Remember, a big goal is actually made up of subsidiary goals that lead to the big goal, just as a big belief is made up of smaller assumptions that lead to that big belief. Change these elements.

Another thing you can do is **to redirect your resources**. Maybe the reason you failed is because of the fact that you did not give it 100%. You've split your attention and your resources between two or more projects. Maybe this is your opportunity to redirect some of your resources to where they need to go so you can achieve greater success.

Regardless of which of the above options you choose to go with, you need to allow yourself to get pumped up by your setback. Because when you allow yourself to get engaged by your setback and excited by it, this proves you are trying. You're not screwing around, you're not just hoping and wishing, you're actually trying.

Also, since the disaster hit so hard, it also indicates that you're making progress.

Because, think about it, if it hurt this much, it means that there was a lot at stake. You have put in a lot. You have gone quite a way. You have sacrificed quite a bit. Whatever the case may be, you were making progress. I know it hurts right now, but this is a good sign because it shows that you have gone quite a distance. This didn't happen right after the gate, otherwise, it wouldn't hurt this bad.

Finally, you have to wrap your mind around the possibility it's only a matter of time until you achieve a breakthrough.

Learning the Right Way

I know I mentioned earlier regarding your disappointment fallback position that you have to choose to learn. Everybody can say that, but the problem is, most people just go through the motions. They say, "Yeah, yeah, I need to learn", but they never learn.

You have to **be systematic and methodical on how you learn**. It's one thing to choose to learn and then stumble your way forward with none of the lessons really sinking in. That's not going to help you. You will find yourself having to relearn the hard lesson again and again until it finally sinks in.

So how do you learn the right way? First, be systematic and methodical regarding what you learn. This means you pay attention to how things happened. You dissect what actually happened.

What is the lesson? Is it what you think it is? Or does it seem similar to something else? Or are you just reading a lesson into this and you're basically clueless? These are three different things. Pay attention to how things played out and get to the core of what really happened. Sometimes things are not what they appear. You might actually be presented with a lesson that you choose to be unaware of. You may even be reading the wrong lesson into the facts.

Another way you can learn is to **think in terms of alternatives**. When something happens and leads to a dead end, what are the alternatives? Look at how things played out and the actions you took. What other alternative actions could you have taken that may have led to a different outcome?

You should also think of **better resource management**. Have you been efficient with your time? Is there a way to get more results from your investment of time, effort and focus?

You should also look into **linking the different lessons that you have learned**. Maybe with this setback, you learn one key lesson. Well, you shouldn't just focus on that and assume that it's floating out there all by its loncsome. Chances are, it's connected to other things you should be learning. Maybe you should link these lessons together. You probably learned several lessons in the past, how was this recent revelation related to the things you already know?

Regardless of how you go about learning the right way, you still have to allow yourself to get pumped up and excited that you have learned something new. This way, you don't get so depressed and so discouraged that you start doubting yourself. In fact, you might find yourself in such a deep emotional hole that you just want to quit. Allow yourself to get pumped

up that regardless of the fact that you lost,
you did not lose the lesson.

Chapter 9: Self-Sustaining Daily Mechanisms To Stay On Track

****

"One small crack doesn't mean that you are broken, it means that you were put to rest and you didn't fall apart"

~Linda Poindexter

Analyze your major daily activities in relation to your big goal. You have to make this a habit. When you sit down to take care of your daily to-do list, always ask yourself, "*How does this get me closer to my big goal?*" This should be the key filter you ask yourself on a consistent basis.

Look at what you learn every day basis and how it can produce seeds or tools that would enable you to reach your big goal. The great thing about doing this is that you not only remind yourself of your big goal, but you keep drilling it into the daily fabric of your life. Your major daily activities do not escape linking with your big goal.

Keep in mind that the fit may not be obvious. It might not jump at you at first, but the more you analyze your major daily activities, the closer you'll be able to make the association.

Spot Daily Wins and How They Relate to Your Big Goal

People achieve something every day. Now, it may not be that big of a deal to other people, but it can be a big deal to you. Look for your daily achievements.

Again, this does not have to be dramatic. You don't have to be some sort of hero. It can be something as basic as taking care of your to-do list and knocking them all out. It can be something as basic as finishing a report that you've been procrastinating.

Whatever the case may be, identify these and ask yourself, "How did this experience help me get closer to my goal?" Put in another way, "Is there anything I learned from this achievement that would help me get closer to my big goal?"

Spot Daily Challenges and How Overcoming Them Relate to Your Big Goal

You can also do this in reverse. You can also look at how your daily challenges can help you stay focused on your big goal. At the very least, you can see how your solutions to your daily challenges can help you get closer to your goal.

Do you spot any changes you need to make? Can you brainstorm any solutions that will help you get out from under your daily challenges? See how these can relate to you achieving your big goal.

The Key

When you're always looking at your daily activities, achievements, victories, defeats, and challenges from the perspective of your big goal, your goal gives you meaning and purpose. It seems that every step you take is in relation to your goal. Every move you make has something to do with your goal.

This is crucial for grit building, because not only do you realize, in a very practical day to day way, that you always have a choice over the things that happen in your life, but it also reminds you your goal gives you meaning and purpose.

Ultimately, this is all about allowing yourself to get pumped up by the fact that you have something you're working for. There is a purpose to you waking up every single day. There is a point for you solving problems so you can go on to the next one and the one after that. You have a personal north star.

This is crucial for building grit because nothing is set in stone. You're not just going through the motions. The results are not predestined or foreordained. You are actively in the mix. You have something to say about your destiny.

Chapter 10: 7 Best Practices to Maximize Grit

****

"Only those who will risk going too far can possibly find out how far one can go."

~ T.S. Eliot

You have so far learned the power of belief and how you should be consistently working toward strengthening your beliefs. You realized the importance of incorporating the bigger picture of your goals into your personal identity as well as the ways to always keep yourself on track despite setbacks and adversities coming in your way.

Now in this final chapter of the book, you'll learn some of the best practices that will maximize your grit. In your journey to build gritty grit, you will find these practices very resourceful. Let's get started.

Best Practice #1: Hang Out With People Who Share the Same Beliefs as You

Try to find out and hang out with people who have the same beliefs or attitudes regarding their goals as you. In other words, they look at their goals as their personal north star. They look at their goals as giving them a sense of meaning and purpose. These people have similar attitudes. They have similar assumptions as to how to realize their goals. They also are focused as intently as you. When you hang out with these people, you get pumped up by their stories. You get excited by their victories because their achievements relate to your journey.

Instead of feeling envious or comparing yourself to them and asking, "why are they so successful and I'm a loser", you get pumped up because you are going through the same journey. Your destinations are different because you have different goals, but you are on the same road.

That sense of fellowship, camaraderie and a shared overall purpose is very comforting. At least you don't feel lonely. At least you don't feel like you're this crazy person who's just out to shoot for the stars, and everybody else is just looking at you wagging their heads and thinking you're a fool.

When you hang out with your friends, you see people who are going through the same journey. You're comforted by that fact. You can draw strength from that fact.

You may find like-minded people in your local meet up groups. If you've not tried earlier, find the like-minded people by hovering over www.meetup.com which is an online platform that connects people and thereafter people can physically meet periodically. Meetup.com is available in big cities in most of the countries.

However, don't fret if you find it difficult to meet people physically in the real world. You can follow people online and listen to their thoughts, so you keep yourself aligned toward your goals.

Best Practice #2: Hold Yourself Accountable

Even if you have a very vivid big goal and it seems almost like some sort of live movie running in your mind, unless you set a timeline, nothing's going to happen. Deadlines push people to get off the fence. They push people to snap out of analysis paralysis and actually take the bull by the horns and take action. Similarly, you should also be clear about signs that you have gone off track. Maybe you should write this down, maybe you should keep this in mind, but you have to be aware of the signs that you have lost sight of your big goal.

Once you're aware of these signs, allow yourself to feel really bad when you go off track. Tell yourself that you're responsible for not setting up the timelines for your goals or not following through to meet the deadlines. This way, an alarm bell or a red flag goes off in your mind when you stray from the big goal and enables you to keep pushing toward that goal. Don't ever get into the trap of blaming other people, economy, as the reason for your inaction –

it's nothing but your mind adopting a victim's mentality. Sometimes things might be out of control, but even in those situations you've to take charge of your life and not get carried away. You have to take the best actions, based on your judgment and the situations at hand.

You might get redirected, you might have to take a detour, you might even have to stop for some time, but the big goal is still there and it continues to call you. It continues to be part of your identity. Therefore, keep your eyes on the long-term goal, and keep taking actions, because that's the only way forward, when you're driven by your passion and true north. And that's what builds and strengthens your grit.

Best Practice # 3: Apply ABCDE Principle to Change Perspective in Adverse Situations

As you know and might have already experienced, life keeps on unfolding always in unexpected way and not always in a pleasant manner. Sometimes despite your best efforts, it turns out, that you fall flat on your face, and maybe start losing hope of achieving your goal. But as you know very well by now developing grit is a marathon and not a short sprint. Therefore, you have to develop mental skills to overcome such situation. Keep in mind that more than often, it is only change of perspective that changes the entire scenario. As once rightly said by Charles Swindoll:

"Life is 10% what happens to me and 90% how I react to it."

Here comes the role of **ABCDE Model** that will help you to look at the things with a new perspective.

This technique is based on Rational Emotive Behavior Therapy, developed by psychologist Albert Ellis initially as ABC Model meaning **Adversity, Belief**, and **Consequences**, and later on expanded by renowned psychologist Martin Seligman by adding D and E to this model – D for **Disputation**, and E for **Energization**, thus coining it as the ABCDE Model.

The ABCDE Model is a step by step question to counter your negative beliefs when you encounter any adversity. This will help you to change your perspective when you're already pushing yourself hard to stay on track. Below is how this model works:

Adversity – This is the problem part – Here you need to describe a recent adversity or a bad situation as an objective statement.

Belief – Next is to record your belief about the adverse situation. Take a note of what you were talking in your head in the face of adversity.

Consequences – Now note down what you were likely to do in that situation based on your instant beliefs. What did you feel or what did you do because of it?

Disputation – Now starts the solution part. Argue with yourself about your beliefs. Dispute your beliefs. Find evidence against your belief or put it into a different perspective.

Energization – Now notice the change in your thoughts and feeling, when you successfully challenged your negative behavior. how did you feel after you have disputed your beliefs?

Let's try to understand this with a practical situation.

Adversity – You started a new venture and suffered losses.

Belief – You will think you don't have business acumen, and should quit the business and go to normal 9 to 5 job.

Consequences – With above belief, you'll feel worthless and start feeling sorry for your decision of starting up – aggravating the problem by feeling worse about it.

Disputation –Now you change the gears. You'd remind yourself that you've already got good work experience, and this loss is just a one-off instance. You'd recall how you had got accolades for your expertise in the domain you started business.

Energization – By Disputing your belief, now you will feel much better about you, your past experience and skill sets, you've developed. You'll tell yourself that you shouldn't quit merely due to such temporary setbacks. Now this will help you jumpstart and take the next decision to turnaround your business.

Next time you encounter an adverse situation and find it difficult to handle, use the ABCDE model to change your default responses and generate positive behavior and actions.

Best Practice #4: Keep a Goals Journal

Keep a journal as you work your way through your goal. Clearly define your ultimate goal. Break it down into sub-goals. Break down those sub-goals into steps. Create timelines for each of the steps. Write down your notes as you go through your goals.

Believe it or not, writing down your goals increase the likelihood that you would be able to achieve them. Simply writing down your goals makes them more likely to happen. So write them down and, just as importantly, break them down. Make them as clear to yourself as possible. Write daily notes regarding your progress on the steps to these sub-goals, which lead to bigger goals, which ultimately lead to the big goal.

Best Practice # 5: Follow the Hard Thing Rule

Angela Duckworth, the researcher on grit, suggest one great rule to build you grit. She calls it "The Hard Thing Rule".

The hard thing rule is basically a daily ritual where every single day, you've got to do a hard thing. Every day, you're going to do a hard thing, because that's how you build grit. You don't build grit by doing things that are easy, or convenient, or comfortable. You don't build grit that way, because building grit is like building a muscle. Can you build your body muscle by lifting a lightweight that you can lift a hundred times, without any feeling of fatigue? Of course not. You build your muscle by pushing yourself beyond what your current comfort zone is, what's currently within your limitation. You push beyond that, and that's how you get stronger. That's how you grow.

Building grit works on the same premise; every day, you're going to do something that's hard. You're going to do something that's outside your comfort zone. It could be going to the gym and push yourself a little bit further. Actually making your workout a hard workout so that you grow and you develop that grit. You got to push yourself past it.

As a writer, the hard thing for me is to push myself to writing up a certain number of words every day, then increasing the word count, or reading a certain number of pages from great books. The hard thing for you could be working an extra hour to deliver that report, which is due tomorrow. Or it could be running half a mile extra, as compared to the previous day.

It could even be meditating a little bit longer. Pushing yourself. Getting past 5 minutes, or 10 minutes, and trying to control your thoughts. That can help build up your grit.

It could be doing something that you're scared to do. Maybe it's getting up in front of a camera and speaking. Every day, you're building your grit.

Best Practice # 6: Adopt Flexible Thinking Patterns

As the saying goes your thoughts become your world. Therefore don't allow your thinking to be rigid. Don't think that there is only one way of thinking rather try to put yourself into shoes of others. Try to understand others perspective. The message is to improve flexibility in your thinking.

Being less rigid in your thoughts and actions allows resilience and grit to blossom. Simply because flexible people don't see problems they see opportunities for growth and learning. When every challenge is met with enthusiasm and creative thinking, you will see yourself as capable and this confidence breeds resilience.

Best Practice # 7: Follow 40% Rule to Build Mental Toughness

Gritty people need to be mentally strong as it is their mental toughness that keeps them put on the track despite facing challenging setbacks and adverse situation. United States Navy's Sea, Air and Land teams, commonly known as Navy SEALs, are one of the most feared soldiers in the world due to the level of their mental toughness that they build during their arduous training.

If you don't know, one of the important ways, in which the Navy SEALs are trained mental toughness is through a rule called the 40% Rule. They are told in their training programs that whenever they feel the first sign of fatigue, it's not the real fatigue – rather it's only the first emotion tiredness generated by their mind. Instead, they are trained that when they get the first signal it means they've just consumed 40% of their energy, and are still left with 60% of their energy to keep going further.

It means even if your mind starts giving you the initial signals that you are tired, you still have a lot inside of you to continue regardless of that. That's why the below quote from Muhammad Ali, the boxing world champion exemplifies this rule. He said: *"I don't count my sit-ups, I only count them when they start hurting."*

All the high-performing athletes know the first wave of fatigue is not the real physical limit of their body. They know with enough motivation, they can transcend this limit. Once you follow this rule, you optimize your chances of building grit, because after all, grit requires you to keep taking action despite any adversities, and obstacles coming on the way.

Closing Thoughts

****

"True grit is making a decision and standing by it, doing what must be done. No moral man can have peace of mind if he leaves undone what he knows he should have done."

~ John Wayne

Now you've gone through the process of building grit. As I have said in the introduction of this book, grit is crucial to success. In fact, it explains success and achievement better than IQ, connections, class background, initial wealth, and other traditional explanations for achievement.

And the best part about grit is that it is a choice. As long as you believe that your ability to learn is not set in stone and that it's OK to fail as long as you try again, grit will see you through. By staying focused on the big picture, regardless of how many detours, setbacks, and bumps on the road you run into, you eventually will get there.

Please understand, however, that your life is not going to change if you just read this book. If you just wrap your mind around the concepts I've shared with you, your life is not going to be dramatically different.

You already know what will change your life? Action. It's one thing to read this book, it's another to carry it out. You have to put the stuff you learned in this book to practice. You have to start.

Now, please, do not allow your mind to play games with you. Don't tell yourself that you will start only when things are just right. Don't kid yourself into thinking that you will get going when you feel that it's the right time. Don't base your actions upon the right kind of feelings. Tomorrow will never arrive unless you make it come.

So you have to set a timeline. I suggest that you don't set it too soon because this would probably intimidate you and freak you out.

You might lose all motivation because it just seems so big, immense and awful that it saps your energy. By the same token, you don't want to set it so far into the distant future that other more pressing issues get your attention. And by the time the deadline comes, you're still unprepared.

Instead, focus on something in the middle. Set a date. Commit to it. It doesn't matter what you feel like when it happens, do it. It doesn't matter if things are falling apart or there are all sorts of emergencies, just do it.

Here's the secret. When you're building grit or working toward any goal for that matter, you don't have to come out of the gate looking like a champion. You can barely limp out of the gate. You can take baby steps, and that's OK. Why? Well, regardless of how small, hesitant and tentative your initial steps may be as you work your way forward, they're still steps forward. But the key lies in taking action, as Martin Luther King Jr. rightly pointed out:

"If you can't fly, then run. If you can't run, then walk. If you can't walk, then

crawl. but whatever you do, you have to keep moving."

So take action now. I wish you nothing but success and happiness.

Your Free Gift:

Did you download your Free Gift already?

Click Below and Download your **Free Report**

Learn 5 Mental Shifts To Turbo-Charge Your Performance In Every Area Of Your Life - in Next 30 Days!

You can also grab your FREE GIFT Report through this below URL:

http://sombathla.com/mentalshifts

DISCLAIMER

While all attempts have been made to verify the information provided in this publication, the author does not assume any responsibility for errors, omissions, or contrary interpretations of the subject matter herein.

The views expressed are those of the author alone, and should not be taken as expert instruction or

75193223R00087

Made in the USA
Middletown, DE
03 June 2018